Quick & easy

Zebra Finch Care

DISCARD

Nikki Moustaki

Photo Credits

I. Francais: 57
M. Gilroy: 13, 20, 25, 31, 34, 49, 51
Eric Ilasenko: 42, 45
Horst Mayer: 32, 58
M. Roberts: 55
John Tyson: 4, 11, 39

T.F.H. Publications
One TFH Plaza
Third and Union Avenues
Neptune City, NJ 07753

This book has been published with the intent to provide accurate and authoritative information in regard to the subject matter within. While every precaution has been taken in preparation of this book, the author and publisher expressly disclaim respon-sibility for any errors, omissions, or adverse effects arising from the use or applica-tion of the information contained herein. The techniques and suggestions are used at the reader's discretion and are not to be considered a substitute for veterinary care. If you suspect a medical problem, consult your veterinarian.

Library of Congress Cataloging-in-Publication Data
Moustaki, Nikki, 1970-
Quick & easy zebra finch care / Nikki Moustaki.
p. cm.
Includes index.
ISBN 0-7938-1020-5 (alk. paper)
1. Zebra finch. I. Title: Quick and easy zebra finch care. II. Title.
SF473.Z42M68 2004
636.6'862–dc22
2004015752

www.tfh.com

Table
of Contents

You and Your Zebra Finch

Congratulations on your decision to bring home a zebra finch! You're in popular company. The zebra finch, also called the chestnut-eared finch, the spotted-sided finch, and the Nyi-Nyi (in the Aboriginal language), is the most widely kept finch in the world, and the third-most kept companion bird in the world, just behind the canary and the parakeet.

Zebra finches make joyful little companions who will usually come to recognize and appreciate a human who is patient and kind with them. A tame zebra finch might even want to perch on your head or shoulder or be petted by you, though most zebra finches do not want to be handled. They are not really "trainable," unlike most parrot-type birds. However, a single finch can develop a strong bond to his owner, perhaps wanting to share his owner's dinner (like any parrot), and many learn to come when called.

Natural History

The zebra finch's scientific name is *Taeniopygia guttata castanotis*, which, roughly translated, means "chestnut-eared grass lover." There is a subspecies called the Timor finch (*Taeniopygia guttata guttata)*, which occurs in Indonesia, about 200 miles off the coast of Australia. This subspecies, also called the Lesser Sundas finch, lacks the barring on the chest that the common zebra has and isn't as well known in American aviculture as is its close cousin.

Zebra finches are originally from the arid Australian Outback, but the zebra finch that comes to live in your home was bred in your country of origin, not imported from the wild. The zebra finch is prolific in captivity and has been bred for hundreds of years.

Characteristics and Behavior

Because the zebra finch makes an ideal scientific specimen, being hardy, easy to keep and breed, and occurring in healthy numbers in the wild, it has been studied more than any other finch. More is

Lifespan

A zebra finch can live 5 to 12 years or more with appropriate care, housing, and diet. A zebra finch that lives into the double digits is one that is being cared for with the utmost concern. Because this bird is often an afterthought in many homes, they tend to only reach three to five years old. Breeding females tend to have the shortest lifespan, which is why it is best to be certain that a breeding female has no more than three or four clutches of chicks per year.

known about its habits, song, learning patterns, and genetics than just about any other bird.

Size
The zebra finch is tiny, though it is not the smallest of the finches. Both males and females are about four inches in length. Some breeders have made this bird larger through selective breeding, especially in Europe, where these birds are shown regularly in competitions. In the US, the size of the zebra finch is more equivalent to the wild zebra finch.

Color
This bird gets its name from the zebra-like stripes across its neck and chest, and especially from its black-and-white barred tail. The "normal" coloring refers to the most commonly occurring color, the color that occurs in the wild, also called the "nominate color." A male with normal coloring has a gray head with chestnut ear patches, black-and-white teardrops at his eyes, bright-red rouge patches on his cheeks, and a bright-red beak at maturity. His abdomen is white and his chest has fine black-and-white barring, with white spots on his chestnut-colored flanks. His back and wings are grayish-brown, with a white rump that merges into a zebra-striped tail. The female is more muted in color, with her beak a paler orange than the male.

Zebra finches come in a variety of mutations, including pied, fawn, cream, white, and many others. If you have a flock of these little guys, it's a good idea to buy several of the different mutations—that way you can tell the pairs apart. However, if you pay close attention to your birds, you will be able to tell them apart even if they are very similar in appearance. Like people, each individual zebra finch has slight differences in appearance or personality.

Zebra Finch Song and Vocalizations
A lot of scientific study has been made on the zebra finch's song and

Dream Singing

Scientific evidence proves that birds, even zebra finches, sing in their sleep. The "dream singing" is a rehearsal of sorts, helping the bird to excel at a variety of songs. A scientific team from the University of Chicago discovered that sleeping birds fired neurons in complex patterns similar to those produced when they were awake and singing. Songbirds store a song after they hear it; then practice it later in their sleep. Scientists believe the songs of birds could reveal how people learn speech.

on the bird's learning patterns in general. Scientists have found that young zebra finch males learn to sing from a "tutor," usually their father. If no tutor is present, the young males will not learn to sing. Learning to sing is important for zebra males, who use their song to attract a mate. The female chooses the male with the most intricate song and is able to do so in about 10 to 15 minutes. In fact, juvenile zebra finches sing more than three times as much as their older

Male zebra finches have a pleasant song that most owners enjoy. Healthy zebra finches of both sexes vocalize frequently, making numerous "peeps" and "beeps" throughout the day.

male counterparts, which sing about 400 times daily. It is suspected that the young zebras are practicing their song.

Much of a zebra finch's other vocalizations sound like happy chitter-chatter. A healthy and happy zebra finch will be quite noisy; a silent bird may not be well. You will also hear a lot of "peeping" or "beeping" from your pair. They sound like tiny car horns. They vocalize all day if they're happy, but they're not loud, and their voices are quite pleasant. The males sing primarily in the morning and less so in the evening. If you are able to keep them outside or by a window where they can hear other birds, they often respond to the wild birdcalls.

Considerations Before Buying a Zebra Finch

Zebra finches bring joy and happiness into millions of homes, and they can bring the same to yours if you are understanding, patient, and are acquiring the zebra finches for the right reasons. Do your

Intelligence

For having such a tiny skull, the zebra finch is no birdbrain. This little bird is intelligent and able to recognize the people and things in his life. Each zebra finch is an individual with his own tastes and ideas about things. Occasionally, you can convince a zebra finch of something, like eating a certain food, but there are things you will never be able to convince him of, like when it's the right time to take a bath. He will decide that on his own time.

A lot of scientific study has been done on the learning capacity of zebra finches, particularly on how they learn song and how they choose mates. This information isn't necessarily applicable to the average zebra keeper, but it is nice to know that your birds have more going on in their little heads than what's for supper.

homework and find out what zebra finch ownership is all about before you buy a pair.

Are Zebra Finches Right for Your Family?

If you're an adult and you want zebra finches for yourself, you're off to a good start. Zebra finches are well suited to adult human companions, and they are not starter pets. Zebra finches and an adult human can have a wonderful long-term relationship. They make great family companions.

If you're buying zebra finches for a child, realize that you might be the one who ends up taking care of them, even if the child promises to feed them, water them, and clean them every day. More often

Responsibilities

Here's a short list of the many responsibilities that you take on when you have zebra finches:
- Daily cleaning of the cage
- Weekly, a more thorough cleaning of the cage and surrounding area
- Offering fresh water twice a day
- Offering and changing fresh foods daily
- Watching closely for signs of illness and taking your zebra finches to the veterinarian if you suspect something is wrong with them or in the event of an injury
- Finch-proofing your home so that it is a safe place if you allow your finches outside of their cage
- Watching other pets closely when the birds are out of the cage (if you allow them out)
- Making sure the cage is out of drafts and that it doesn't get too cold or too warm in the room in which they live
- Checking the cage and accessories daily for wear-and-tear.

than not, the parent assumes responsibility for the birds soon after they are brought into the home. It's fine to obtain zebra finches for children as long as you are prepared to handle many of the responsibilities that come with ownership.

Beside the cage and the birds themselves, you will need to buy other supplies for your finches, including perches (several types and sizes), nest boxes, and cups for food and water.

Expenses

The first expense you will incur is the zebra finches themselves. Then you'll need all of the other add-ons to get started, like an adequate cage, cups, and perches.

Next, there's the necessary expense of visits to the avian veterinarian. Your birds should see an avian veterinarian for a checkup within the first few days of their homecoming in order to ensure that they are healthy and also to establish a relationship with the doctor who will treat them in cases of illness. Many people bring in fecal samples to the veterinarian once or twice a year to make sure that the birds are well. This is easy—just put wax paper in the bottom of the cage overnight, and the next day you'll have plenty of samples for the vet.

You will also have to spend money on food, accessories, and occasional treats every month.

Responsibilities of Zebra Finch Ownership

Your zebra finches rely on you for all of their needs—proper housing, nutrition, health care, and safety. You are responsible for every aspect of their lives.

Expect to spend at least a 15-minute-a-day minimum caring for your birds, more on the days when you're doing a more extensive cleaning. That's a commitment of at least three hours a week, possibly more. Luckily, owning zebra finches is more a pleasure than a chore.

Mess

You will definitely have a crunchy seed-scattered floor and perhaps even a bit of water to go with it, no matter how often you clean the cage. You might even find seeds growing out of your carpet if you're not a great housekeeper. Even if you buy all of the seed-catching devices and all of the hooded cups on the market, you are not going to prevent mess, so be prepared for this.

Choosing the Perfect Zebra Finches for You

If you feel that zebra finches will fit into your lifestyle and that you

Timeline of the Zebra Finch

- Incubation (the time the parents spend sitting on the eggs): 14 days
- Fledging (when the babies start leaving the nest): 21 days
- Eating independently: 35 to 45 days
- First molt (losing "baby" feathering and coming into adult coloration): approximately 35 days
- Complete adult feathering: approximately 60 days
- Full size: approximately 3 months
- Breeding maturity for hens: 3 months (but you should wait at least six months to allow them to breed)
- Breeding maturity for males: 3 months

and your family are prepared for the expenses and responsibilities involved in zebra finch ownership, you can now move on to selecting the right zebra finches for you.

How Many?

A single finch can become quite lonely, and because these are not typically "hands-on" birds, a pair is the norm. Because they are generally kept in pairs, your zebra

Zebra finches are social birds, so it is best to buy them in pairs or small groups. A single zebra finch is likely to be lonely and stressed.

finches will not need you to keep them company. Merely play the radio softly while you're out and talk to them when you're home. Most people keep two or more zebra finches, generally in male/female pairs. This way your zebra finches can keep themselves entertained and occupied, and you won't have to worry about a single finch alone at home pining away for a companion.

Age

The zebra finch ages remarkably fast. By the time a zebra is three months old, he is able and ready to breed (though it is inadvisable to breed zebra finches before six months of age).

A fledgling is a young bird that has just come out of the nest and is able to eat on his own. This is the best time to get zebra finches if you want them to be tame. Most baby zebra finches are eating well on their own at 6 to 8 weeks of age and can be taken to a new home at that time. Some breeders might want to wait a little longer before they sell the babies to make certain that they are strong and healthy.

There are two good ways to tell the age of your new zebra finch. First, the best way to determine the bird's age is by studying the leg band: A closed band is generally put on by the breeder when your zebra finch is about eight days old, and usually has the breeder's initials, state, and the month and year in which the zebra finch was hatched engraved on it. This is the only real way you can be certain of your bird's age.

You can also make a good estimate of the bird's age by studying his coloring. A juvenile zebra finch is grayish-white, has a black beak, and has black teardrops under his eyes before he has come into his adult coloring. Some mutations are brown as juveniles, and some are white. However, once this bird molts into his full adult coloring at about three months of age, it's going to be hard to tell whether the bird is a year old or five years old if he doesn't have a leg band on.

The Colorful World of Zebra Finches

Zebra finches come in more than 30 mutations, and more are being developed all the time. Even so, you will probably find only a handful of these distinct mutations in your local pet shop. There is no difference in the companion quality among the different colors.

The wild zebra's base color is gray/brown and is the base color from which all of the other colors were developed. Those other colors are called "mutations" and are natural occurrences finch breeders capitalize on, breeding those mutated birds to each other, assuring that the mutation will appear again.

Where to Find the Right Zebra Finch

A local pet shop should have a cage full of zebra finches, all ready to go home with you. Look for a shop where the employees seem to know about birds and will take the time out to help you and answer questions.

If you're very lucky, you will find a zebra finch breeder, someone who breeds for mutations and for showing, who is serious about the hobby, and who can help you find the best zebra finches for you. A reputable breeder will be able to give you references you can call before you go to see their birds. This way, you can be sure it is safe to go to their homes, and you can be assured of the quality of their birds. No matter where you obtain your zebra finches, ask for a health guarantee and the right to return your zebra finches should something go wrong.

How to Choose a Healthy Zebra Finch

There are several initial things to look for in choosing a healthy zebra finch. Nevertheless, once you buy your zebra finches, you should make a well-bird checkup appointment with your avian veterinarian just to make sure they're healthy, especially if you have other birds in the house that may contract any diseases your new finches might bring in to your home.

First, pay attention to the bird's eyes. A zebra finch's eyes should be round, clear, and bright. There should be no crust or discharge from the eyes, and the eyes should show an attitude of alertness. The nares and cere should be clear as well. A zebra finch's nostrils are called nares, and they are located on the cere, which is the fleshy part just above the beak. The nares should be clean and without discharge. The cere should not be crusty or peeling.

Next, notice the bird's feathers. The feathers of a healthy zebra finch are shiny and tight, lying flat against the body. A zebra

A healthy zebra finch is active and vocal. When selecting a new pet finch, take your time and choose the healthiest one.

finch with excessively ruffled feathers may be ill. The exception to this is the finch that is housed with other finches that may have picked on it and pulled some feathers out. Other than this case, the feathers should cover the whole body—if you notice bald patches, the zebra finch may have a problem.

A zebra finch's feet should be free of debris. The zebra finch should be able to perch easily on both feet. Sometimes a zebra finch becomes crippled and can have splayed legs or other foot problems—this is no reason to turn him away. A crippled zebra finch still has his wings and will be able to get around if allowed full flight.

The vent is underneath the bird and is the place where waste is eliminated and where the eggs emerge in females. The vent should be clean, not crusty with feces or other material.

Finally, a healthy zebra finch will have a good attitude. A healthy zebra finch is active and chattery and always on the move. A zebra finch that is sitting on the bottom of the cage, fluffed and sleepy, might be having a problem. Try to choose the zebra finch that is hopping around the cage socializing, eating, and bathing.

You might be tempted to buy the sleepy, sick-looking bird. If you do, you risk infecting your other birds, you'll incur huge veterinary bills, and the bird might not survive anyway. Better to start out with a healthy bird that will cause you the least worry.

Hand-Raised or Parent-Raised?

Occasionally you can find hand-raised finches, finches that were removed from the nest at a young age and fed a formula through a spoon or syringe by a human caretaker. In the case of a hand-fed zebra finch, you'll have a finch that's bonded to humans and will be perfectly comfortable with you. Never try to force a parent-raised finch to be "friendly," because you will only result in terrifying him.

Housing Your Zebra Finch

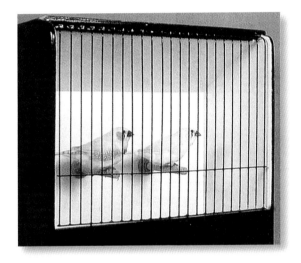

As you may have noticed, there are many types of cages on the market. Some of them are even labeled for finches, though the general fault in finch cages is their size. Which one to buy?

The housing decision might seem obvious to you. Perhaps you want a certain color, or you have budget restrictions. While these things can influence your decision, they should not, by any means, be the sole deciding factor in buying a cage. Remember, this is your finches' home, the place where they may spend considerable time.

Cage Size

Though finches are small, they need very large cages—the bigger, the better. A pair of zebras confined to a small cage will be very, very unhappy. Working the flight muscles keeps the bird healthy, active, and strong. Vertical flight requires the most effort and gives the greatest exercise, though horizontal flight is good, too. All zebra finches need frequent exercise, and breeding females in particular can suffer greatly if not provided with enough exercise.

Even though a cage is large, however, it may not be good for zebra finches. Make certain that the bars of the cage are not wide enough for the birds to stick their heads through—this can be dangerous. Square or rectangular cages are far better than round cages because they offer more cage space for the same basic cage size.

Cage Materials

Most cages are made of metal and plastic, and some are coated to add a color or a texture. Make sure that the coating on the outside is non-toxic. If you notice that your zebra finch is picking away at flaking coating, *remove the bird from the cage immediately* and get a new cage that does not have faulty coating. Ingestion of this coating can be deadly.

Think of practicality and comfort first and the cosmetics last when you are looking at cages. A "pretty" cage is not always the best or

Wide, Open Spaces

A large cage is great, but if the cage is so full of accessories—perches, toys and swings—that you can hardly find the bird inside, you might be crowding the bird out. Finches do like a little variety, but they need room to flap and fly without the fear of hitting something with their wings.

Stick with Plastic and Metal Cages

Wooden cages are unacceptable for zebra finches, though they are often touted as the perfect type of cages for them. Wood is porous and can become damp and harbor bacteria and mites, so it's better to stick with plastics and metal.

safest cage for your zebra finches, nor will it be the easiest cage to keep clean and sanitary. Some decorative cages have metal scroll-work that can catch a toe and cause bleeding, which can be danger-ous for a little bird such as a zebra finch. Look for simplicity in a cage.

You can now buy cages made of acrylic that allow full vision in and out of the cage and practically eliminate mess. These cages are much more expensive than the standard metal cages, are attractive, safe, and can save you some time cleaning. Some even come with mechanical ventilation that cleans the air inside the cage, a nice fea-ture for those who suffer from allergies.

If you choose to purchase an acrylic cage, be sure to place it in an area that doesn't receive full afternoon sun. These cages have a minor problem with temperature changes, as the acrylic sides have the ability to focus the warmth of the sunlight.

Be certain the cage has a slide-out drawer in the bottom, so you aren't required to completely dismantle the cage in order to clean it. Newspaper works best as a cage liner. It is the least expensive mate-rial, and it is an excellent way to recycle your daily read.

It also shows your bird's droppings clearly. Often, signs of illness are apparent in a bird's droppings, so being able to see your birds' droppings is important. Sand or wood shavings absorb or hide the droppings, which would keep you from seeing a possible illness in your bird.

Cover the bottom of the drawer with newspaper to catch your bird's droppings and spilled food. Change the paper daily.

Cage Accessories

Cage accessories are a non-negotiable part of owning a zebra finch. However, shopping for cage accessories is the fun part, and it might even become one of your favorite pastimes.

Perches

The cage may have come with a few plastic perches or a few wooden dowels. Even though these are good perches, they are an inadequate selection by themselves. Because your zebra finches use their feet so much, it's important to have perches of many different widths, materials, and textures on which to stand. If your birds only have one type and size of perch to stand on, they can develop serious foot problems. Think of good perches as orthopedic shoes—they can make a world of difference when it comes to your bird's happiness and health.

Natural wood perches look nice in a finch cage and are good for your bird's feet. If you use perches collected from outdoors, be sure that the wood comes from a nontoxic tree and that you clean and disinfect them before use.

You can make perches from your live trees outside, but you must be absolutely certain that the type of tree is nontoxic and that it was never sprayed with insecticide or fungicide. Fruit trees, hazelnut, or willow branches work well. Check for unwanted "guests" in the branches. Wipe all branches from outside with a mild bleach solution (10 percent bleach, 90 percent water), rinse well, and dry in the sun. This will remove any fungi or bacteria that might be on the branch from a visit by a wild bird.

If you use rope perches, be careful to trim all loose strands that might fray. These loose strands can wind around a toe, foot, or neck and cause injury.

Concrete perches are available in all sorts of colors and diameters and can often become a bird's favorite perch. This is a rough perch that acts as a nail and beak trimmer. Your zebra finches should have at least one of these perches, but not to the exclusion of other types.

Many people are fond of sandpaper sheathes that slip over existing perches. However, these are not really beneficial for your zebra finch's feet, because they can become moist, are soiled easily, and will harbor bacteria.

Also make sure that the perches are not placed over the food or water dishes. This will help to keep the dishes free of droppings. Don't place so many perches in the cage that your zebra finches can't move around. Leave some space for flying.

Food and Water Dishes

The cage you purchased probably came with a couple of cups for seed and water. These are a good start, but you'll need a few more cups to complete your set, including other types of cups for other food items.

The cups that came with your cage are probably plastic, which is not the finest material for a bird cup. Plastic can become scratched and hold bacteria in the grooves of the scratches, no matter how well you clean it.

On the other hand, stainless steel is a great material for bird cups. It's durable, easy to clean, and long-lasting. Ceramic cups are also a good choice. Both of these types of cups can be found with holders that keep them secure in the cage to avoid seed dumping. There are ceramic cups available with hoods to keep your birds from tossing seeds all over the room.

Watch the birds if you use them, however. Some birds would rather starve than put their heads inside an enclosed space. The same is true of cups that clip outside the cage through a covered opening. If your birds must reach into an enclosed space for their seed, they may not want to do so.

To keep your zebra finch's cage clean and to save your valuable time, consider keeping two sets of dishes. This means that you will have six dishes—two for seeds/pellets, two for water, and two for fresh foods. Each day you should remove the dirty dishes and replace them with the clean ones, allowing you to then disinfect the other dishes for tomorrow.

Millet Holders and Birdy Kabobs

A millet holder is a good, inexpensive investment—this little clip allows you to attach the millet spray to the side of the cage where your bird can work at it. A "birdy kabob" is a great way to get your little feathered pal to eat his greens—simply thread the fruits and veggies onto the kabob and hang it in the cage. This gives your zebra finch the feeling of having to work for his food, something he would do in the wild.

Cage Covers

A cage cover can help prevent night frights, which is kind of like a birdy panic attack. The cause of night frights can be as simple as shifting shadows in the room, a passing car's lights, or the sudden entrance of a person or other household pet. Panic attacks, in which the birds flap wildly and flutter all over the cage, hitting the sides and floor, can cause a great deal of damage. A cage cover can help prevent this trauma.

Tube-style waterers are popular among zebra finch owners because the water often stays cleaner longer in the tube—there is no space for the zebra finch to toss food and droppings into.

However, just because the water lasts longer doesn't mean that you don't have to change it every day. Be certain that your finches are actually drinking from tube-style waterers if you choose to use them. If you change from a cup waterer to a tube, leave the cup in place for a few days until you actually see the birds drinking from the tube.

Mineral Blocks and Cuttlebones

Mineral blocks and beak blocks are essentially a lump of minerals

Mite Protectors

A mite protector can be found in your basic pet shop and looks like a round tin with holes punched on one side. This product contains an insecticide that is rather unnecessary for your zebra finch and can even be harmful. Yes, zebra finches can get mites, but it's unlikely that they will and even more unlikely that a mite protector will do anything to prevent them. Mite protectors are not a substitute for good care and veterinary attention.

shaped into a block, or nowadays, into a fun fruit or vegetable shape. Your zebra finch will appreciate this treat. It will help to keep his beak trim, and it will add some calcium to his diet.

A common accessory, the cuttlebone, comes from the cuttlefish, a kind of squid. This is an important cage accessory, not just because your zebra finch will enjoy working on it, but because it is a good source of calcium as well. Breeding finches will demolish their cuttlebones almost faster than you can provide them, so be certain to have plenty on hand.

Cage Cover

Some zebra finches really like their cages to be covered at night, while others may only want to be covered halfway or on three sides. Covering the cage offers a degree of security and protection, because your bird will not be disturbed from sleep by light in the house or a cat slinking around. The cover protects from drafts as well, and the darkness in the cage may allow you more sleeping time if your bird generally likes to get up with the sun and you don't. Offering a cover is like tucking your birds in at night. Don't cover your birds during the day, however, unless there's something disturbing going on in the environment, like workers in the house or yard.

Toys

Toys for a finch? Sure, why not? These tiny birds like to play as much as larger birds, though the toys you might buy for a larger bird just won't work for your finches. Finches won't chew on wood blocks or rawhide, and they will ignore large toys or toys that need a little work to get them going. They need toys geared to their size and lifestyle.

Most birds love mirrors. However, if you have a male/female pair, be alert to an "attack the intruder" reaction from the male over the other male in the mirror. He may decide to drive the intruder from his cage and become stressed that the intruder can't be forced out.

Finches find swings to be great fun, and so will you, as you watch their antics. Your finches will hop on and off to get the swing really moving. Small ladders can be fun for them, too.

Bird Baths

Bathing is good for your zebra finch's skin and is a natural behavior—even if it's a bit messy! Realize that your bird knows when it's time for a bath and will do it on his own good time. Preventing your bird from bathing is a terrible idea, as is forcing your bird to bathe.

Zebra finches enjoy toys such as ladders and swings, so include a few in the cage. However, make sure you leave your birds enough room to stretch their wings and fly.

Most birds will bathe in their water dish, which will actually encourage you to clean it more often. You can also provide your zebra finch with a separate bath that he may prefer to the water dish, which may be smaller or narrower. A shallow dish or the saucer for the bottom of a flowerpot makes a good "bathtub," as will a jar lid for a tiny bird.

Place the bath on the floor of the bird's cage every other day for a few hours. Do not leave it there all the time, and remove it immediately if it becomes fouled with droppings. If your birds don't seem to want to bathe, try spraying them with a light, warm mist. Some birds prefer a shower to a bath. Don't spray the birds on chilly days, and don't spray too close to bedtime. Give the birds time to preen and dry off before you cover the cage for the night.

Cage Location

Once you've chosen a cage, supplied it with the necessary accessories, and settled your new little family members inside, where should you place your finches' new home? Find a place where the birds are able to see activity, but make sure it is an area that is not too busy. Too many people going by, boisterous children, or racing dogs and cats will exhaust the poor finches. You need an area that is quiet but not too secluded.

Be certain the cage isn't easily available to curious small children or to your dog or cat. Place the cage where it will get plenty of natural light, and avoid drafty areas or areas where there are excessive temperature changes.

The kitchen is one of the worst locations to place a cage. Not only will the birds be in an area where there is too much activity, but they will also be exposed to smoke from cooking, as well as toxic fumes from non-stick cookware. When heated, the material that coats non-stick cookware gives off fumes that can—and will—kill a bird. Therefore, never use non-stick cookware or appliances around your zebra finches. In fact, it may be best only to use cookware that isn't made with non-stick material.

Toxic Fumes

Your tiny friends have a sensitive respiratory system. The fumes given off by heated non-stick cookware are not the only dangers to your zebra finches. Fumes you might not even notice can be deadly for your birds. These include scented candles, air fresheners, and even perfume. Try to keep the air in your zebra finches' environment as clear and safe as possible.

Lighting

"Bird-Proofing" Your Home

If you plan on letting your finches fly free for any period of time, you need to first "bird-proof" your home so that it is safe for your finches. The average home is actually quite dangerous for birds, so it's important to take the necessary precautions so your zebra finches can safely enjoy time outside of the cage. It is also recommended that you supervise any time your zebra finches spend outside of the cage.

Common Household Dangers

First and foremost, make sure that any predators (your dog, cat, ferret, or snake) do not have access to your birds *at any time*. Lock them in another room while the birds experience the freedom of flight. Other, larger birds, like parrots, can also be a danger if the finches land on their cage. Tiny feet might get nipped and injured badly.

Be certain that children (and immature adults!) do not try to catch them in midair, and be careful to look before you step or sit down. A bird can land on the floor directly in front of your feet or on your favorite chair without notice. Be aware of your flying friends' locations at all times.

Draw your drapes or pull your curtains closed to cover the temptation of a window. A finch might fly into the glass, seeing the wide world outside. The same is true of mirrors.

Cooking foods, pots of boiling liquid, and pans of oil (even cool oil) can all spell disaster. Cover them before the bird is allowed to fly. A bird that lands in a bubbling stew or pot of spaghetti sauce does not have a great chance of survival.

Likewise, if your zebra finches fall into an aquarium or into a sink full of dishwater, they will certainly need rescue. The same is true of your toilet–close the lid. Occasionally, birds have also been known to fall into a glass of liquid like water, soda, or a cup of tea, so make sure any containers of liquid—no matter how small—are covered whenever your zebra finches are out of the cage.

It might sound as if you should never allow your finches to fly free, but they can, with care. A small room with a closed door is ideal. If you are certain all possible dangers are removed, and you keep an eye on your flying adventurers, there will be no problems while they explore their home.

An outdoor aviary housing zebra and other finches makes a beautiful and interesting addition to a home. Aviaries require quite a bit of planning and expense, but the result is usually worth it.

Safe Cleaning Supplies

Many household cleansers are deadly to your birds, so don't use them in or around your birds' cage. Instead, use natural disinfectants, such as vinegar, for cleaning the cage and baking soda for scrubbing.

If you have a real mess, you can use a 10 percent bleach solution for soaking, which will kill any bacteria or viruses in the cage, but make sure to rinse very carefully.

Apple cider vinegar is a very good disinfectant as well. It will help to purify your birds' water, as well as help to keep your birds healthy. Just two tablespoons of apple cider vinegar to a gallon of water will be excellent for your bird's drinking water.

If you cover your birds at night, wash the covers with a mild, unscented detergent and dry either on the line or without a toss-in fabric softener sheet. Always be certain detergents and fabric softeners are unscented if you're using cloth around your finches

Aviaries and Bird Habitats

A better alternative to a cage is an aviary. An aviary is a very large cage that houses one or more zebra finches, usually a few pairs. Zebra finches enjoy one another's company if there's ample room. If not, fighting can ensue.

If the aviary is very large, you can house other mild-mannered Australian birds in it as well—cockatiels, parakeets, Bourke's, and some other varieties of finches. Over the last few years, many retirement homes and nursing facilities have installed aviaries. The residents find the antics of the tiny birds enjoyable and soothing.

You can create an aviary in the backyard of a large home or in the living room of a small apartment. You can order an aviary from a catalogue or buy one from a large bird-specific shop.

An aviary should be large enough to fit a human adult inside of it. People often build indoor aviaries out of wood and plastic sheets or Plexiglas. The Plexiglas keeps the mess inside, but still allows you to see the birds and their environment.

In the warmer states, a backyard aviary is ideal. As long as the outside temperature doesn't drop below 45°F, an outdoor aviary will work well for zebras. One facet of an outdoor aviary difficult to replicate indoors is the ability to have large, growing plants and trees for the birds' pleasure. Be certain the plants and trees you choose are non-toxic. The birds need an area in the aviary where they can find shelter from bad weather, as well as plenty of nesting areas.

A habitat is an aviary taken to the next level. It's usually larger and contains natural elements, such as plants and running water. Some zoos have habitats, and they are becoming popular with bird fanciers as well. The idea of a habitat is to recreate, as closely as possible, the animal's natural environment. Yes, it would be quite difficult to recreate the Australian grasslands, but at least allowing your Zebra finches to fly and interact with nature—the sun and the weather—is a start. Because most habitats are kept outside, there are considerations such as predators and foul weather to contend with, but a well-built and well-planned habitat can withstand these hazards.

Zebra Finch Nutrition

In the wild, zebra finches eat primarily grass seeds. They are also opportunists, more than happy to eat bugs and to scratch around in the soil for anything consumable. By doing this, they get all of the nutrients they need to thrive. The seeds provide carbohydrates and protein, the bugs provide protein, and the soil provides minerals. Though you may not be able to provide the same diet zebra finches receive in the wild, you can easily provide a diet that consists of most, if not all, of the nutritional elements that your finches need.

A good finch diet should consist of seeds, sprouted seeds, vegetables, fruits, and live food. There is also a breeding diet, which

Finches relish millet sprays, and millet can comprise a large portion of your zebra finches' diet. Millet sprays are available at most pet stores.

should include increased amounts of greens, egg food, and live foods. Of course, non-breeding finches will like these treats as well.

Seeds

There are good finch seed mixes available on the market, but you may notice that your birds favor some seeds over the others, which wastes a lot of seed. Selective eating is also a waste of money, but this is easily remedied by preparing your own seed mix.

Millet is the mainstay of the companion zebra's diet. There are several types of millet that you can buy in bulk and mix–white proso millet, red millet, and golden millet, just to name a few. Close observation of your finches should tell you what they like best. Note that finch seed mixes and canary seed mixes differ, and finches aren't wild about many of the seeds in the canary mix. Avoid seeds that are too large or too pointy.

Seeds should be fresh and viable; that is, able to germinate. To test whether or not the seeds you regularly purchase are viable, simply place a teaspoon of seeds on a moist paper towel and set them on the windowsill. Keep the towel moist, and in a couple of days, at least 90 percent of the seeds should sprout, if not more. If your seeds don't sprout, that means they're "dead" and don't have the nutrition that viable seeds do. In that case, change the source of your seeds.

Sprouted Seeds

Sprouted seeds are high in vitamins, as well as enzymes, proteins, and minerals. There are many good commercial seed sprouters on the market for a fairly low cost. One in particular has three layers of sprouting area and is very easy to grow. However, if you want to make your own sprouter, you will need a few items.

First, you will need a wide-mouth jar, preferably of glass. Start small; then increase the size of your jar as you increase the size of your flock.

You will need a piece of screen or cheesecloth to cover the mouth of the jar. If you use cheesecloth, use a large rubber band to hold the cloth in place over the jar's mouth, or you can cut the center from the jar lid to fit back over the screen of cheesecloth to hold it in place.

Sprouting seed is very simple. Add a seed mix consisting of white millet, proso millet, and/or red millet to the jar to fill it approximately 1/4 to 1/3 full. Fill the jar with cold water and allow it to sit overnight; then drain the water from the jar through the screen or cheesecloth top. Refill with cool water, slosh the seeds, and drain again. Do this approximately 10 to 12 times.

Grit

Grit is important to your finches' digestion, and some kinds of grit, such as oyster shell grit, add calcium to the diet as well. You can find grit easily in any pet shop. Include a small dish of grit in your finches' cage at all times. Vary the types of grit that you offer. Some finch owners don't use grit at all, and their birds are fine, so it's a bit of a controversial issue. Too much grit can lead to digestive disorders, though most finches don't gorge on it. The fact is, finches do like the grit and can use it, so you might as well offer it, but do so in small amounts, and be sure your finches aren't eating too much.

Slant the jar at a 45-degree angle, with the mouth of the jar over the sink or a bowl, until all of the water has drained. Shake it, lay it on its side overnight, and repeat the wash-and-drain procedure.

By the third day, the seed sprouts will be long enough to feed to your birds. You may refrigerate the sprouts for up to four days, but if they have a bad smell or appear even slightly moldy or slimy, *do not feed them to your birds.* Discard them, and start over.

Fruits and Vegetables

Although zebra finches can live just fine on finch seed mix, they will have a longer, healthier life with a more varied diet. Add fresh fruits—finches love sliced grapes, oranges, and melons. Vegetables do well if you clip them to the side of the cage or thread them through a kabob-type hanger available in most pet stores. Remember, though, that fresh foods spoil rather quickly, so don't leave them in your birds' cage for more than a few hours.

Zebra finches especially like cucumber, baked sweet potatoes, apple, grapes, melon, green beans, greens, cooked carrots or grated carrots,

Provide a varied diet to your finches that includes a wide selection of greens, other vegetables, and fruits. Remove offered fruits and vegetables after a few hours to prevent your birds from eating spoiled food.

Quick & Easy Zebra Finch Care

oranges, and lots of other fruits and vegetables. If they don't like a particular item prepared one way, prepare it another way. For example, offer melon slices, finely chopped melon, and big chunks of melon. You will soon see how your finches like it prepared. Dark-green and orange fruits and veggies are particularly nutritious. Make sure to wash everything thoroughly before offering it to your birds.

Live Foods

Most finches enjoy some live food as a treat now and then. Small mealworms and grubs make an excellent addition to the diet, and you can get them at some pet stores or order them on the Internet. They are usually sold in small plastic containers that you keep in your refrigerator in order to slow down their lifecycle.

If you're not squeamish about insects, you might benefit from raising your own mealworms. Mealworms are very high in protein. The chicks in the nest grow quickly and need all the nutrition they can get, but when your adult finches aren't breeding, don't let them gorge on live foods. A few grubs a week as a treat will do when there are no eggs to produce or chicks to feed.

Ants' eggs, which are sold frozen, are also available. You can also get earthworms, maggots, and wax-moth larvae. Maggots should be placed in an open container filled with bran so they can clean themselves internally and externally before you feed them to your birds.

Eggs

Hardboiled eggs are a great protein and calcium source. Be sure to boil the eggs for at least half an hour to kill any bacteria that may be in or on them. Crush the egg, shell and all, and offer in a separate cup, leaving it in the cage for only a few hours — you don't want any food to spoil while the birds still have access to it.

When you eat eggs yourself, don't toss the shell away; instead, microwave it or boil it for a few minutes, crush it up, and offer it to the birds. This is a welcome treat and very high in calcium. It is especially great for breeding females who need the extra minerals for egg production. You can add some whole-grain cereal or toasted wheat germ and a bit of Spirulina to chopped egg and serve it to your happy flock.

Home-Cooked Foods

Cooking for your zebra finches? Yes, people actually cook nutritional treats for their birds. One really easy recipe requires that you do little more than turn on the oven and watch the clock: zebra finch muffins. Simply buy an in-the-box corn muffin mix, prepare it using the directions on the box, then add nutritious items that you know your birds like—for example, eggshell, chopped broccoli, spinach, and so on. If your birds are reluctant to eat it, try adding some millet seeds next time and they may be tempted to try it.

Austerity Diet

The austerity diet is a method used to convince zebra finches (and other birds) to breed by imitating conditions found in the wild. During the rainy season, when heavy rains produce an ample supply of food, the zebras are stimulated to breed. However, during the rest of the year, food is only plentiful enough for the adults, not for hungry chicks in the nest. The finches will put off breeding until the rainy season arrives again.

If you're breeding your finches, you can mimic their natural instincts and stimulate them to breed when you choose. At the outset, offer your birds plenty of protein daily, such as live food or egg food. After about a week, set them up for breeding by adding a nest and nesting materials. After two or three clutches, remove the nest and cut back on the excess protein (don't eliminate it, but don't offer it every single day). When you want them to breed again, you can start over.

Signs of Vitamin Deficiency

 Your finches need vitamins, just like you do. The following are some signs that your finches might not be getting what they need:

- Vitamin A Deficiency: Soft-shelled eggs, bone deformities, skin lesions, poor plumage. Feed more dark-green and orange fruits and veggies.

- Vitamin D Deficiency: Soft-shelled eggs, rickets, incoordination, staggering gait, egg binding. Feed hemp seed, ground sunflower seeds, cooked egg yolk, cod liver oil.

- Vitamin K Deficiency: Inability of the blood to clot. Anemia. Feed broccoli, kale, and other green veggies.

- Vitamin B1 Deficiency: Diarrhea, retarded growth. Feed wheat germ and whole grains.

- Vitamin B2 Deficiency: Fewer eggs, lack of coordination, weakness, poor plumage, curled toes. Feed spinach, chard, asparagus, and other green veggies.

- Niacin Deficiency: Skin lesions, poor plumage, diarrhea. Feed greens.

- Folic Acid Deficiency: Poor feather production, anemia, retarded growth. Feed lentils, collard greens, chick peas, papaya, broccoli.

- Vitamin C Deficiency: Weakness, blood-clotting problems, deficient immunity. Feed oranges, apple, kiwi.

- Calcium Deficiency: Soft-shelled eggs, eggs that do not hatch, little to any egg production, egg binding. Supply your birds with extra calcium, particularly during breeding, with cuttle bones, oyster shell, and crushed hard-boiled egg, shell and all. A diet high in cereal grains, spinach, beet greens, or chard may interfere with calcium absorption (as these do in humans as well). These plant products have other healthful properties, so don't eliminate them, just make sure that your birds are getting enough calcium.

However, in general, most zebras will love it. Cut up the muffins and freeze them, then each morning warm one in the microwave (don't serve hot!) and give it to your finches.

There are many foods available in pet shops or on the Internet for your birds that are simple to cook, tasty, and very nutritious. Cooked grains of all kinds, like barley, couscous, or buckwheat groats, are also popular.

Offering the occasional piece of angel food cake or pound cake is a good idea, because it can be easily soaked with vitamins or liquid or powdered medicine, making them much easier to give to the birds. Once the birds are used to this occasional treat, they won't notice that there's something added—well, hopefully they won't.

Water

Clean water should be available at all times. Check your birds' water several times a day, not only to be certain there is plenty, but also to check for contaminants. Some birds like to make their own "soup," putting seeds, fruits, and vegetables into their water. Others manage to get their droppings in the water dish, which is even worse. A water bottle or tube will solve those problems, but be certain your bird is using it. Don't remove other water supplies until you see the bird actually drink from the bottle or tube.

If your tap water isn't of the best quality, you would be well advised to purchase bottled water for your birds. Even if your tap water is clean, additives such as chlorine are not in your birds' best interest. A simple water purifier is helpful, especially one that guarantees removal of chlorine and other contaminants. Apple cider vinegar added to the water helps to remove bacteria and is good for the birds. Add two tablespoons of vinegar to one gallon of water and store in a cool place.

Zebra Finch Health Care

The first and most important facet of keeping your finches healthy is having a relationship with an avian veterinarian, a doctor who specializes in the care and treatment of birds. Birds are obviously quite different from dogs and cats, and need a special physician trained in the particular treatment of bird accidents, ailments, and diseases. A veterinarian that does not specialize in birds may not catch a subtle symptom of illness or may not perform the proper tests.

The best place to find an avian veterinarian is by calling the Association of Avian Veterinarians at (561) 393-8901or looking them up on the Internet at www.aav.com. You can also get a reference from the store or breeder from whom you obtained your zebra finches, or you can contact a trusted veterinarian in your area.

Illness Prevention

The most important information you can learn about caring for the health of your zebra finches is that prevention is the best policy. Hygiene is extremely important in preventing and controlling outbreaks of disease. Many illnesses are spread through feces and dirty water or contaminated food.

Be certain the cage, perches, toys, dishes, and anything else in your birds' area are clean. Scrub food and water dishes daily, or run them through the dishwasher. Scrape and scrub perches as they become soiled. Change the paper in the cage bottom daily. Keep the area

Your First Avian Vet Visit

You should take your new finches to an avian veterinarian within three days of buying them. There are several good reasons for doing this.

- If you bought your zebra finches with health guarantees, you will have some recourse if tests reveal that your new birds are ill.

- You will begin a relationship with the avian veterinarian who will get to know your birds.

- Some avian veterinarians will not take an emergency patient unless the bird is a regular client.

- Avian veterinarians often board birds in their offices, though some will only board clients—that way they can be relatively sure the bird will not bring diseases into their office.

- You will receive important recommendations from the doctor regarding diet and housing.

around your birds dry. The main cause of fungus is moisture, and fungus can be deadly. An air purifier is also a good investment.

Quarantine

If you are introducing new birds into your flock, quarantine them for at least 30-40 days. Quarantine means to separate the birds fully from any other birds in the house. This allows the new birds to show any hidden illness they might be carrying. Care for your news birds last, after you tend to your other flock.

Do not overcrowd your zebra finches, as overcrowding will cause your birds stress. Additionally, it is much more difficult to keep a crowded cage clean.

If you handle the new birds or their accessories, always wash your hands and change your clothing before handling other birds. Take stool samples to your avian veterinarian to check for potential illness. Watch the birds carefully for any symptoms. The quarantine period also allows the new birds to adjust to a new environment.

Anatomy of a Healthy Zebra Finch

It is necessary to understand the appearance and behaviors of a healthy zebra finch in order to recognize symptoms that could indicate illness. While every zebra finch is an individual, and some traits that are abnormal in one bird may be perfectly normal in another, there are many general characteristics true to any zebra finch that indicate a healthy, thriving bird.

Eyes and Vision

A zebra finch has one eye on either side of his head, allowing him to see almost 360° around his environment. This helps him watch

A wise keeper quarantines a new bird for at least a month before adding him to an established flock. This helps prevent introducing diseases to the healthy birds.

for predators and other dangers. Birds also have a second eyelid that acts as a kind of squeegee for the eye, keeping it moist and clean.

A healthy eye is clear and moist and free of discharge. A zebra finch with an eye problem may squint or scratch it excessively with his foot or will rub it on the perch or sides of the cage. Look for swollen eyelids, cloudy eyes, excessive blinking or discharge, and tearing.

Ears and Hearing

Your zebra finch's ear is located a short distance parallel from the eye and is covered by feathers. You may get a glimpse of it after your zebra finch bathes, when the feathers around the head are wet and stuck together. Birds can't hear in the range that we do, but they can hear in greater detail. If you can see your zebra finch's ear opening when the bird isn't wet, make an appointment with your avian veterinarian.

Feet

Zebra finches' feet have three toes in front and one in back. They should have no deformed or malformed toes or nails. The scales on the legs and feet should be smooth, not crusty, and should have slender feet and toes. Thick feet with heavy crusts are a sign of mites or other disorders. The bird will hold up a damaged foot and favor it, causing the bird to have a possible problem with balance and landing.

Feathers

Feathers are one of the most amazing, functional parts of a bird, helping him to fly, regulate temperature, and repel water. A healthy zebra finch should be obsessed with taking care of his feathers, preening them for much of the day. A zebra finch likes to keep his feathers neatly "zipped," clean and well organized on his body. Preening functions to keep the feathers neat and coats the feathers with oil that the bird will pick up from his "preen gland," located at the base of the tail.

Birds molt about once or twice a year, usually when sunlight becomes shorter or longer. Molting is when a bird loses some of the old feathers on his body and grows new feathers. When your zebra finch molts, you will notice feathers on the bottom of the cage, but you should not be able to see patches of skin on your bird—if you do, there could be a serious medical problem.

Respiratory System

Your zebra finches have very delicate respiratory systems that are sensitive to airborne irritants, such as aerosol sprays, fumes from heated non-stick cookware, and tobacco smoke. Birds don't breathe

Molting

Molting birds go through a cranky time. Their skin might itch, and the new feathers breaking out of their skin may even be painful. Molting is seasonal, but for birds living inside, away from the seasons, it can occur any time. Molting can last a few weeks to a few months.

A molting bird will appreciate a bath or a misting offered daily, perhaps with a little aloe vera juice mixed in with the water. The bath will help to soften the sheathes over the pinfeathers and will help the feathers emerge.

the way we do. We inhale and exhale, completing one breath. Birds have to take two breaths. The first breath fills the air sacs, located in hollow spaces in the body and in some of the bones, and the second breath pushes the air into the lungs.

Birds are prone to respiratory illness and distress because their system is more complicated than ours. If you notice your zebra finch panting, call your avian veterinarian. Also, always be sure to keep your zebra finch away from fumes and airborne toxins.

Musculoskeletal System

Birds are fantastic athletes, and as a result, tend to be well muscled. Many of your zebra finch's bones are filled with air, and all are thin-walled, which makes them light—this is a necessary development for flight. Though bird bones are strong enough to allow the movement of wings in flight, they are easily broken. If you suspect that one of your zebra finch's bones is broken, take him to the veterinarian immediately.

Digestive System

Although a bird doesn't chew his food the way humans do, he does crack seeds, swallow, and send the food into the crop, which is just below the bird's neck and near his breast. Food is then partially digested in the crop, then passed on to the stomach (proventriculus), then on to the gizzard (ventriculus), where it is ground very fine, then passed to the cloaca, which collects the feces and urates before being eliminated through the vent.

Signs and Symptoms of a Sick Zebra Finch

Now that you know something about healthy zebra finches, it's important to know the signs or symptoms of illness. If your zebra finch usually greets you when you come home from work with a concert of singing and beeping, and one day that doesn't happen, you can be sure that something is going on with your bird.

Perhaps someone in the house has moved its cage, something has frightened it, or the temperature has dropped or risen too much—these are possibilities. If you can't find any reason for the unusual behavior, you should start looking for the following:

- Fluffed feathers
- Sleeping too much, or sitting on the bottom of the cage
- Loss of appetite
- Attitude change, and allowing you to handle him (lethargy)
- Lameness
- Panting, labored breathing, or tail bobbing with each breath
- Discharge from the eyes, nostrils, or vent
- Food stuck to the feathers around the face
- Feces around the vent (diarrhea)
- Discolored or bloody feces. Your zebra finch's droppings should consist of a solid green portion, white urates (on top of the green), and a clear liquid. If any of these are discolored (darker green, black, yellow, or red) and there has been no change in diet, there might be a problem.
- Scaly feet
- Drooped wings and shivering

Common Zebra Finch Ailments

There are many common ailments that zebra finches suffer from, but it is important to remember that only your avian veterinarian can truly diagnose an illness. If you suspect that one of your zebra finches is suffering from any of

The ruffled feathers of this fawn zebra finch could be a sign of illness. Awareness of your finches' normal behavior and appearance allows you quickly to detect signs of illness and distress.

the ailments listed, take your companion to his avian veterinarian immediately.

Parasites

Mites

The tiny feather mite is not common in zebra finches, but can infest birds that live outdoors in unsanitary conditions. Red mites eat their host's blood, are highly contagious, and can cause anemia in your bird, though they are not very common in zebra finches. Scaly, crusty feet in your bird is a possible sign of mites.

Air Sac Mites infest the trachea, lungs, and air sacs of a bird and can lead to suffocation and death. These mites are spread from parent to chicks during feeding, and can be transmitted to other adult birds by the infected bird coughing and sneezing. Other birds are also contaminated through the food and water. Symptoms include heavy breathing, coughing, sneezing, open mouth breathing, stained nostril feathers, singing cessation, and incessant wiping of the beak on the perch.

Yeast

Yeast infections, or candidasis, affect the mouth, digestive tract, and sometimes the respiratory system. Your zebra finch normally has a certain amount of yeast in his body, but when his bodily balance is abnormal, as when he's undernourished or after a treatment of antibiotics, the fungus can grow to excess.

A zebra finch with a yeast infection will have a sticky substance in his mouth and may have white mouth lesions. Regurgitation and digestive problems may occur.

Offering your zebra finch foods that are loaded with vitamin A, such as green leafy vegetables and orange fruits and vegetables, can help prevent yeast infections.

Eye Problems

Causes of eye problems range from foreign objects in the eye to cold drafts and fumes in the room. However, some eye problems are a symptom of infection, including bacterial infections, respiratory infections, mites, and conjunctivitis. If the eye is caked shut, try bathing it with a warm saline solution, being very gentle as you hold the finch, and making sure not to get the solution into the respiratory tract. If this does not help, contact your avian veterinarian.

Giardia

Giardia is a one-celled protozoan that can affect your zebra finch, but it can also affect other animals in the house and even you. Giardia is passed by contaminated food or water. You may notice diarrhea, itching, an inability to digest foods, weight loss, and other symptoms.

Worms

Tapeworms, roundworms, and gizzard worms occur in zebra finches, and can cause obstruction in the digestive tract and even death.

Coccidia

This parasite causes extreme weight loss in finches—they eat, but they still lose weight. Young birds are particularly vulnerable. The good news is that this disease can be prevented in young finches by treating the parents for it before the chicks hatch. See your veterinarian for the proper medications.

Infections and Disease

Aspergillosis

Aspergillosis is a fungal infection that causes respiratory distress and can be deadly. Any changes in your zebra finch's breathing, changes in vocalization, or gasping or wheezing can indicate this infection. Prevent this infection by keeping your zebra finches' environment very clean and dry, and avoid corncob and/or walnut shell bedding.

Tuberculosis

Mycobacterium avium is responsible for the tuberculosis infection and can be transmitted in food and water or by unsanitary housing. Avian tuberculosis can be transmitted to humans with compromised immune systems. Symptoms in a bird include weight loss and digestive disorders.

Psittacosis (Parrot Fever)

Psittacosis, also called *chlamydiosis* and parrot fever, is also transmittable to humans, and causes respiratory distress symptoms in both human and bird. Psittacosis is transmitted through droppings and infected secretions. Some zebra finches can be carriers of the disease without showing any symptoms.

Polyoma Virus

Polyoma virus usually affects young zebra finches, which die around

Stress

Stress is one of the leading causes of lowered resistance to illness; the second is a poor diet, though that can lead to stress as well. Your birds need to feel secure and know that they can escape from predators. The presence of a cat or dog, especially if the animal is able to get close to the birds' cage, is extremely stressful.

Stress can be caused by excessive noise, such as construction on or near your home. Disturbances at night, which keep the bird from getting enough sleep, are also stressful. An obese bird that doesn't get enough exercise is also at risk for stress.

the time of fledging. This disease occurs mainly among breeding stock, though households with many birds are susceptible. There is no treatment for polyoma virus, so prevention is essential.

Pacheco's Disease

Zebra finches enjoy splashing about in a birdbath. However, they frequently will defecate in the water, so clean and disinfect the bath after each use.

Pacheco's disease is a virus that affects the liver. This disease is fatal and is mainly diagnosed upon death, which comes rapidly. This is a highly contagious disease. Always enforce strict quarantine.

Reproductive Disorders

An egg-laying hen that hasn't had enough calcium in her diet may have eggs with soft shells that will be difficult to lay, resulting in egg binding. This can also occur when the egg is malformed, or if the hen has a tumor or other disorder of the reproductive system. Symptoms of egg binding are panting and lameness, among others. Keeping the laying hen fit and nourished will help to prevent this problem.

If you can't get to your avian veterinarian right away, you might be able to help a hen pass an egg by adding a few drops of mineral oil (or olive oil) to the vent (where the egg comes out), and giving her a few drops in the mouth with an eyedropper. Then place the hen in an incubator that provides heat and humidity.

Grooming

Believe it or not, regular grooming is essential to your zebra finches' health. Zebra finches love to bathe, and it's a real treat to watch them happily splashing away in a birdbath.

There are many kinds of birdbaths on the market, and none are superior to any others. There's a shallow type of bath that hangs on the outside of the cage and allows the bird to enter and splash around with a minimum amount of water spilled outside of the cage. There are also types with mirrors on the bottom that seem to be quite popular. A shallow dish or the clean saucer from a potted plant often makes a satisfactory bathtub as well.

Many zebra finch owners use misters or spray bottles to bathe their birds. Remember to use tepid to warm water and encourage bathing in the daylight hours so that the bird doesn't go to sleep wet.

You might not think that a bird bathing in winter is a good idea, but your bird might insist! Your home may be very dry in winter, and he may need to moisten his skin. Birds generally know what's best when it comes to bathing, so trust his instincts. There's no need to blow-dry or towel-dry your zebra finch, but you should provide a warm lamp to dry under.

There are bathing products that you can buy in the pet shop that claim to have certain properties that are good for a bird's skin and feathers. Most of these products are unnecessary and may even irritate your zebra finches' eyes. Read the labels and use your best judgment, or save your money and use good old-fashioned water.

Breeding Zebra Finches

A zebra finch is a highly adaptable little bird that will breed easily. However, this is not a decision that should be taken lightly. In fact, most people should *not* breed their zebra finches. Breeding is a serious decision that produces living, breathing birds that will need homes and loving care.

Things to Consider Before Breeding

First and most importantly, you need to consider where the babies will live. Do you have enough space, time, and resources to house them yourself, or do you have other people willing to provide forever homes for all of the babies? If not, you should not breed your zebra finches.

Telling male zebra finches from females is fairly easy. A mature male zebra finch has a bright orange or red beak and orange patches on his cheeks.

Female zebra finches are more dull in color than the male. A female's beak is pale orange, and she lacks the bright cheek patches of the male.

Second, you should consider whether or not you can afford to breed your zebra finches. Many people assume they will make money from breeding, but in actuality, it can be expensive. Veterinary costs, food and housing expenses, and other supplies can become quite expensive in the long run, so you should be certain that you can afford all of the necessities involved with breeding.

Finally, time is a necessity. If you don't have the time to provide the extra care and attention necessary, you probably should not breed your zebra finches.

If you do, in fact, have the time, money, resources, and potential homes for the babies, and you have carefully made the decision to breed your zebra finches, you can have a successful breeding plan if you follow the correct steps and go into breeding fully prepared.

Breeding Requirements

First of all, be sure that you have a true pair. Finches are sexually dimorphic, which means you can tell the male from the female by looking at them. The male zebra finch sports a black breast bar, has chestnut flanks speckled with white, orange cheek patches, and a bright red beak. The female zebra finch does not have the markings of the male, and her beak is a softer, paler shade of orange.

Your birds should be old enough to breed (six to nine months old, at least), should not be related, and should be in top condition. Although zebra finches can—and often do—breed at a younger age, it's in their best interests to wait until they've reached their full maturity. Though they reach sexual maturity at three months, it is inadvisable to breed them then.

The diet of a breeding pair is also extremely important. Be certain to give the hen plenty of calcium in order for her to produce eggs with strong shells and to prevent egg binding. During egg production, your little hen will leach calcium from her own body and bones to supply her eggs. The breeding pair also needs eggs, egg food, and live food at this time (you can skimp on the live food, but try it if you can).

Breeding Cage and Nests
The cage should be large enough for the birds to exercise in and shouldn't be crowded with things that prevent flying. If you can, cover the cage on two sides to give the couple a sense of security. Place the cage in a low-traffic area to prevent disturbance. Provide a broad spectrum of light shining on the cage or allow the birds to have some sunlight daily (but don't let them get hot).

There are more than a few types and sizes of finch nests available. Zebra finches aren't really picky about their nests and will often nest in just about anything they can fit inside. They have been known to nest in the bottom of milk cartons, inside tin cans, and in flowerpots. However, you will probably want to use one of the more popular finch nests, such as a bamboo woven nest that's available at any pet store.

The wooden nest box sized for finches is also popular. It can be set inside the cage or hung from the outside. The wooden boxes are easy to clean and make it easy for the breeder to check on eggs and chicks as they grow.

Nesting Material

Short grasses, such as hay, make a great nesting material. Short string does as well. Fibers such as jute, coco fiber, and sisal can be used, too—the birds will build their nest to their liking if you offer a variety of materials. Avoid material such as synthetic fibers, hair, plastic shredding, or cut up grocery bags or tissue paper. Offer nesting material clipped to the side of the cage or on the bottom, but not where it can be soiled. If you offer material that's too long, it may get wrapped around a foot or neck, and the finch may get stuck in the nest. Watch your finches carefully to make sure that each individual leaves the nest each day.

Adding the Birds

Put your two birds in either a split cage with a divider or in two small cages, side by side. Once it's clear that they like one another and have begun to bond, you can place them in a larger cage. Look for the male's "song and dance" routine as he sings and tries to woo the female. If she approves of him, you may notice her raise and fan her tail.

It's a good idea to clip your birds' toenails slightly prior to breeding to prevent damage to the eggs. After that, let nature take its course, and don't check up on the pair too often. If they are disturbed, you run the risk of the pair abandoning their eggs or offspring, though zebras are pretty good parents in general. Check no more than once a day to ensure they have fresh food and clean water, and a quick peek for eggs.

Egg Laying

Your zebra finch hen might pluck her chest area bare when she's ready to lay her eggs, and will line the nest with the feathers. The nest requires a nice, soft lining, and the eggs need her body heat to incubate properly—with the bare chest, the heat will not be filtered through feathers. You can help her by saving molted feathers for breeding time and offering them to her while the pair is building the nest.

If you breed your zebra finches, you must provide them with a suitable nest. Commercially available finch nests are usually made of bamboo or woven grass; most pairs accept these nests quite readily.

She will lay between four to seven eggs in the average clutch, usually one every other day. After the third or fourth egg has been laid, incubation begins. The parents will share egg-warming duties, taking turns while the other is out of the nest to eat and drink or to get a little exercise. At night, both parents sleep in the nest.

Hens lay between four and seven eggs on average, spreading out the laying over a few days to two weeks. Both parents will spend time sitting on the eggs.

If the eggs are fertile, they will seem to darken after the first week. You can "candle" the eggs to be certain of their fertility. Candling is a relatively easy procedure. Purchase an "egg candler" from a pet shop or online. This is a flashlight with a very long wand at the end that concentrates light at the tip.

Wait for a moment when the parents are out of the nest, and gently stick the candler's wand into the nest, letting the tip rest gently on each egg (don't move the nest while you do this, and don't touch the eggs). If the egg is at least five days old and fertile, you will see a webbing of red lines, or possibly even a small red dot inside a larger dot. This is the chick embryo. Once you have candled the eggs, check to see if the parents are still tending to them. Offer them something they like, such as live foods, to get them back into their routine.

About 12 to 14 days after the hen has begun to "sit tight" (incubate), the eggs will begin to hatch.

Zebra Finch Chicks

The chicks will hatch in the order in which their individual egg was laid. The body is pink skinned, covered with light-colored down, and is about an inch long. This varies depending on the mutation of the birds. Chicks grow rapidly, and feather out by the time they're 16 days old. At around 18 days, they begin to venture out of the nest. During the next 14 to 21 days, the parents continue to feed them, with the father taking on most of the feeding duties. He also begins to teach his sons their song (well, he sings and they listen).

At about this time, the parents are ready for another clutch of eggs, and might begin to chase the young out. The fledglings are now ready to be removed from the parents' cage to prevent feather plucking (or worse) by the parents. Feed the youngsters the same diet you feed the parents, but go heavy on the soft foods.

Emergency Care

Occasionally, zebra finches will abandon either their fertile eggs or their chicks, and sometimes a chick falls out of the nest (or is kicked out). If this happens, there's still hope for the babies. If there's another pair sitting on eggs, you might foster the abandoned eggs with that pair by adding the eggs to their nest. Society finches are best known for fostering and readily accepting foreign eggs and chicks, but zebra finches will foster as well. Try to keep the eggs to no more than six or seven under a sitting pair.

You can also try to foster an abandoned baby with another pair, which often has good results. Sometimes you may have to try to feed the baby yourself. It's very difficult, time-consuming, and generally not successful, but it's not impossible. Using an eye dropper and commercial baby bird food that you mix and warm up, gently feed the baby one drop every 15 minutes during the day, and every hour at night. As the baby grows, you can allow more time between feedings. Don't ever feed the baby too much at one time, because he can choke on the food and die. As the baby gets older, offer

Zebra finch eggs hatch in about 12 to 14 days. The chicks hatch without feathers, but they will be completely feathered out in about 16 days.

Chicks are always hungry. Both parents will spend much of their time feeding the ravenous brood.

seeds and other foods in the cage so that he weans off of hand-feeding.

You will need to keep the baby in a brooder, and, if you have more than one chick you're hand-feeding at a time, you might want to invest in a commercial version. The Styrofoam models aren't very

If a chick falls out of the nest, the parents usually will care for it. If not, you will have to feed and raise the baby yourself, a difficult but not impossible task.

expensive. However, you can create a homemade brooder very easily. You will need a glass aquarium with a hood, such as one used for tropical fish. Cut a hole in one end of the hood. Line the aquarium with a layer of newspaper and a few paper towels. Fill a tall, sturdy glass container with water and place it in the aquarium, beneath the hole you cut in the hood. Insert a fish tank heater into the water-filled container and set the heater's thermostat to medium. Put an outdoor thermometer inside the tank to check the temperature. Do not let it go over 98°F for a young chick.

Place the newly hatched chick into a small, shallow Tupperware dish lined with shredded paper towels, and place it in the center of the tank. You must be absolutely sure that the water-filled container cannot tip over–if it does, it may drown the chick. Another version of the brooder uses a heating pad beneath half of the tank, which is safer.

As the chick feathers out, drop the temperature in the water container or heating pad (and thus the tank) until it reaches room temperature by the time the chick is eating on his own. By then, the chick will have hopped out of the Tupperware dish and will huddle against the base of the water-filled container (or heating pad side of the tank) if he's chilled, or will hop away it gets too hot.

If an older youngster, one having a few feathers and moving around on his own, has fallen from the nest, leave him out of the nest (but with the parents) but watch him carefully. Generally, the parents—particularly the father—will attend to him.

At times, zebra finch parents will bicker and fight with one another. If this happens and continues, it would be best to remove one of the adult birds for a short while, perhaps a day, and then try returning him to the nest again. They will often calm down after the short

If your zebra finches abandon their offspring, you can place the eggs or chicks in a society finch nest, a species well known for raising the young of other finches.

Breeding Zebra Finches

separation, and will return to normal behavior. If the fighting continues in spite of all attempts to settle their argument, you will have no choice but to remove one of the adult birds and leave the other to raise the chicks as a single parent.

Over-Breeding

Occasionally, a breeding pair will not want to stop production after three or four clutches of chicks. This will deplete the calcium of an egg-laying hen, as well as deplete the strength of both parents. It is necessary to convince them to stop breeding and rest for a couple of months.

Remove anything that might stimulate the birds into breeding, such as a nest, nesting materials, or anything they might use for nest building. Cut back on their protein. Feed them egg food no more than once a week, and stop any live food if you have been feeding it. Keep them away from other pairs with chicks. The cries of the hungry chicks arouse the breeding drive. If these measures fail, separate the birds for a short time.

Breeding for Exhibition

Zebra finches are one of the most exhibited finches. Bird shows are quite fun to attend and are a real learning experience.

There is no recipe for instant success in breeding show-quality birds. A breeder must learn to assess the potential of breeding stock and recognize desirable and undesirable features in order to produce the best possible young. With experience, a breeder is able to recognize the merits of individual birds with ease. Note that the most expensive birds are not necessarily those best suited for exhibition. Price is not a good yardstick.

When you're breeding for showing, record all breeding results and band your chicks with numbered rings. Be prepared to work long and hard in order to get those show winners. Remember most of all that breeding zebra finches is a hobby and should be enjoyable. Try joining a club where other fanciers share their experience and expertise. Some mutations of this unique little bird can be a serious challenge to even the most capable bird breeders.

Zebra Finch Mutations

In zebra finches, a mutation reveals itself as a color or pattern change from the look of the normal zebra. There are more than 30 zebra finch mutations on the market. These mutations are quite fancy, and some of them can fetch quite a price.

Common Color Mutations

Some of the common mutations include the following:
- Fawn
- Lightback
- Chestnut-flanked white
- Black-breasted
- Black-cheeked
- Black face
- Orange-breasted
- Penguin
- White
- Silver
- Yellow beak
- Crested
- Pied

Additionally, there are mutations that are relatively unknown and/or restricted to a limited geographical area. These include the following:
- Cream back (Australian)
- Black Front (Australian)
- Grizzle (Australian)
- Charcoal (Australian)
- Florida Fancy (American; also often called Isabel)
- Light Cheeked (European)
- Agate (European)

There are two mutation varieties of the zebra finch, the dark mutation and the light mutation. Most mutations continue to have a white belly, like the "normal" bird. One of the newest mutations is the black cheek, which look like the nominate bird, with the exception of a black patch where the normal bird has an orange patch. Black-cheek mutations can be bred with other mutations to produce varieties such as silver black-cheeks, fawn black-cheeks, chestnut-flanked black-cheeks, black-cheek black-face, and black-cheek black-breasted.

A particularly attractive mutation of the zebra finch is the penguin. This bird has a dark upper body with black wing feathers edged with silver. Their upper breast and stomach area are white.

The light-colored mutations of the zebra finch are various shades of white, light tan, or cream, and lack the vibrant markings of the darker mutations. The lightest of all zebra finch mutations is the white finch, which retains the orange beak and legs of the "normal" bird, but is devoid of other markings. Unlike the albino, which has no color and has red eyes, the white zebra has dark eyes. True albinos are extremely rare.

Some zebra finch mutations look similar to one another, and all can be crossed, though zebra finch breeders have recommendations on which mutation goes best with another. Breeding for color mutation is an educational experience for both the beginner and the serious finch hobbyist. People often become obsessed with having the new mutation, or developing something original and beautiful. Hopefully, this "finch bug" will overtake you, and you'll enjoy a whole new world of zebra finches.

Resources

ORGANIZATIONS

The Zebra Finch Society
P.O. Box 41414
Lafayette, LA 70504-1414
http://www.zebrafinch-society.org/

Acadiana Aviaries
Garrie Landry
2500 Chatsworth Road
Franklin, LA 70538
(337) 828-5957
E-mail: Garrie@zebrafinch.com
www.zebrafinch.com

South East Queensland Zebra Finch Society
Homepage
Contact: Ellis W. Thornley
5 Bauhinia St
Birkdale
QLD 4159
Australia
(617) 3822 4580
E-mail: ellist@powerup.com.au
http://homepage.powerup.com.au/~ellist/zebra%2
0finches%20of%20australia.htm

Zebra Finch Society of Australia
Contact: Mr. Gordon Kelly
7 Braddon Street
St Marys, 2760 NSW
Australia
Email: gordok20@hotmail.com

Zebra Finch Society
Contact: Gerald Massey
Flaxby
Knaresborough
North Yorkshire HG5 0RR
Tel. 01423 863035
E-mail: zebfinsoc@aol.com

The Zebra Finch Society of Canada
Contact: Sam Crabbe
52 Briarwood Ave.
Mississauga, ON, Canada
L5G 3N6
(905)274-3233

New Zealand Zebra Finch Society
P.O. Box 117
Bunnythorpe
New Zealand
E-mail: Peter+Anne.Russell@xtra.co.nz

MAGAZINES

Finch and Canary World
Seacoast Publishing Bookbag
850 Park Avenue
Monterey, CA 93940
http://www.seacoastpub.com/fcw_mag.html
subcribe at: (800) 864-2500

Australian Birdkeeper Publications
P.O. Box 6288
Tweeds Head South, NSW 2486
Australia
+61 (07) 5590 7777
Fax: +61 (07) 5590 7130
www.birdkeeper.com.au

Bird Talk Magazine
Subscription Division
P.O. Box 57347
Boulder, CO 80323-7347
www.birdtalk.com

INTERNET RESOURCES

Efinch
E-mail: roy@efinch.com
http://www.efinch.com/

Zebra Finches
http://zebrafinch.info/

Finchworld
www.finchworld.com

ADOPTION AND RESCUE ORGANIZATIONS

Finches With Wishes
www.finches.org

The American Society for the Prevention of Cruelty to Animals
424 East 92nd Street
New York, NY 10128-6801
(212) 876-7700
www.aspca.org
E-mail: information@aspca.org

EMERGENCY CONTACTS

Animal Poison Hotline
(888) 2320-8870

ASPCA Animal Poison Control Center
(888) 426-4435
www.aspca.org

Index

Quick and Easy Gerbil Care